A German Regiment among the French Auxiliary Troops of the American Revolutionary War:

H. A. Rattermann's History

Edited by
Don Heinrich Tolzmann

CLEARFIELD

Edited by Don Heinrich Tolzmann
from an unpublished manuscript by
H. A. Rattermann

Copyright © 1999 by
Don Heinrich Tolzmann
All Rights Reserved.

Printed for
Clearfield Company, Inc. by
Genealogical Publishing Co., Inc.
Baltimore, Maryland
1999

Corrected Edition reprinted for
Clearfield Company, Inc. by
Genealogical Publishing Co., Inc.
Baltimore, Maryland
2002

International Standard Book Number: 0-8063-4910-7

Made in the United States of America

Table of Contents

Part One - Editor's Introduction   v

Part Two - Rattermann's History   1

Part Three - Editor's Conclusion   50

Index   56

Part One - Editor's Introduction

Editor's Introduction

For some time, the editor of this work has taken an interest in illuminating the role German-Americans have played in American history, from the beginnings to the present.[1] Among his special areas of interest was shedding light on the German dimension in the American Revolution.[2] With this work, he has edited a previously unpublished manuscript, which deals with the German troops which served in French military units which fought on behalf of American independence in support of the revolution. This manuscript was located in the Rattermann Collection at the University of Illinois-Urbana, and gratitude is herewith expressed for permission to publish this heretofore unpublished work of H. A. Rattermann.[3]

In editing several works on the American Revolution, the editor has brought out various editions dealing with the German-Americans who fought for the Revolution, as well as with the German troops allied with the British cause. However, it is relatively unknown that the French forces which fought for American independence contained German units. The reasons for German units in the French military derive from the aftermath of the Thirty Years War, which left Germany weak and divided. As a result, France pursued two foreign policy objectives, first, to maintain the status quo with regard to German disunity, and second, to obtain a border on the Rhine for military and commercial purposes. Both of these objectives implied direct involvement on the part of France in the internal affairs of the German states in general, and in particular French possession of the German provinces of Alsace-Lorraine. In pursuing these aims, France also set the stage for Franco-German conflict, which would carry on into the 20th century.[4]

As a result of its occupation of Alsace-Lorraine, France then drew on soldiers not only from this region, but from the southwest German realm as well.[5] This, therefore, resulted in the fact that when France came to the support of the struggle for American independence its military forces included German units. Nevertheless, this remains to this day a little known fact of the history of the American Revolution.

What is most interesting about this is that the American forces had German-American regiments and units, but were also assisted by French forces with German units. These forces in turn were pitted in conflict against the British, which also contained German units, most commonly, of course, known as the "Hessians." Hence, to really appreciate the German dimension in the American Revolution, it is necessary to take the following three aspects into consideration: first, the role played by German-Americans in the American Army; second, the role played by German units in the French Army allied with the Americans; and, finally, the role played by the German troops allied with the British Army. Only the constellation of these three aspects fully comprehends and illuminates the German dimension in the American Revolution.

It is known that there were German regiments and units in the American forces drawn from the colonies, especially from Pennsylvania, Maryland, and Virginia. Given the fact that there were also such substantial numbers of German units in the French Army, the suggestion might be made that at least one-third of the American Army was German, and consisted either of German-Americans, or of the Germans in the service of the French.

This particular work does not deal with all the German units in the French forces, but focuses on the particular unit known as the Royal German Regiment Zweibrücken, or Deux-Ponts, which was under the command of the Prince Christian von Zweibrücken.

Gratitude is expressed to Dorothy Young, Department of Germanic Languages and Literatures, University of Cincinnati, for the preparation of the manuscript of this work.

DHT

1. For example, see Don Heinrich Tolzmann, ed., *The First Germans in America: With A Biographical Directory of New York Germans*. (Bowie, MD: Heritage Books, Inc., 1992).

2. See the following works edited by the editor of this volume: *German-Americans in the American Revolution: Henry Melchior Muhlenberg Richards' History*. (Bowie, MD: Heritage Books, Inc., 1992), and *German Allied Troops in the American Revolution: J. G. Rosengarten's Survey of German Archives and Resources*. (Bowie, MD: Heritage Books, Inc., 1993).

3. See Donna-Christine Sell and Dennis Francis Walle, eds., *Guide to the Heinrich A. Rattermann Collection of German-American Manuscripts*. (Urbana: University of Illinois Library, 1979). I would like to not only express gratitude to the University of Illinois Library for permission to publish this work by H. A. Rattermann, but also express special gratitude to Mr. John Hoffmann of the University of Illinois Library for his assistance in obtaining copies of the manuscript. For further information on Rattermann, the well-known German-American historian and editor of the historical journal *Der Deutsche Pionier*, see Don Heinrich Tolzmann, *German-American Literature*. (Metuchen, NJ: Scarecrow Press, 1977).

4. Regarding the French encroachment into German territory, see Don Heinrich Tolzmann, "Understanding the Causes of the German Immigrations: The Context of German History Before 1830," in: Don Heinrich Tolzmann, ed., *Das Ohiotal - The Ohio Valley: The German Dimension*. (New York: Peter Lang Pub. Co., 1993), pp. 3-19.

5. For further information on French military history, see Steven T. Ross, *French Military History, 1661-1799: A Guide to the Literature.* (New York: Garland, 1984).

Part Two - Rattermann's History

Much has been said and written about the German mercenaries, that were brought by Great Britain to this country during the war of independence, to aid in the suppression of the liberties of the colonies, in the struggle, which the fathers of our republic carried on against the tyrannies of old England; and they were certainly not complimentary terms which the indignant people of America bestowed upon the poor wretches, sold by their princes and potentates for the pounds of sterling which covetous "John Bull" was willing to pay for them. Among the epithets that were, with a view of conveying on odious designation, applied to them, the term "Hessian" became most in vogue.[1] With this nickname alike all the German soldiers - those from Brunswick, Ansbach-Bayreuth, Waldeck and Anhalt-Zerbst as well, as those from the two Hessias - were termed, that fought in the British ranks during the said war. By unthinking and coarse people, as well as by a vulgar, unrefined press, this epithet has often been applied to the German inhabitants of the United States in general, even up to our present time. To the latter class of base slanderers I have only to say, with a variation of the poet:

A sensible and well-bred man

Will not insult them, and no others can!

Of the former it may be said that many historians such as Frederick Kapp, George Bancroft, George W. Greene, J. G. Rosengarten, Edward Jackson Lowell and others have furnished satisfactory proof, that injustice has been done them.[2] Capt. Max von Eelking, who has written an extensive history of those unfortunate auxiliary troops, says in the introduction to his book: "Seldom have troops, like these, been placed in a more unhappy position. Fate denied them the advantage, to spend their heroism in a purely national or patriotic cause. If, however, it is to be an accusation of crime, that they obeyed the command of their superiors, like well-disciplined soldiers; that they met the destructive influences of an unaccustomed climate, and shared the dangers and disagreeableness of a mode of warfare, to them entirely unknown; that they contended with and overcame the most perilous obstacles like brave warriors, and remained true to their oath and their flag under the most adverse circumstances; and finally that they vied with an heroic nation in bravery and endurance; if these qualities are to be a reproach cast upon them, then it would be like carrying water in to the ocean, to attempt remonstrances against such arguments. We may decry the principle, that placed these unfortunate troops in such an unenviable position, as a wrong but we must not cast the accusation of guilt upon those, that were simply the tools of a higher power, that rested in yonderdays so heavily upon all classes of the European people."[3]

I repeat: Much has been said and written about these unfortunate Germans, and I have read many and varied authors upon that subject but I have not yet found in any history of the Revolutionary war – excepting only the mere mentioning of a few of the most distinguished officers of the American army, such as the Baron von Steuben, the General DeKalb, Muehlenberg and a few others, and the slight notices of two or three German battalions of the Pennsylvania, Maryland and Virginia line – any mentioning of the fact that there were on the side of the colonies a likewise large and I believe even greater number of Germans, who fought and shed their life blood upon the battle-fields of American independence, and for the liberties of this country, than the number of unfortunate Germans, that were forced to fight in the British ranks. History does not mention a single prominent instance of Germans volunteering in the British army of that war, but on the contrary; all the Germans fighting on the side of the Colonies – excepting those, of whom I am about to speak in particular – were volunteers in the cause of liberty and independence.[4]

In most cases the Germans, that fought on the side of the colonies, are treated, and I say justly treated as Americans, for they were, though of German birth or descent, equally true and heroic American patriots, as their brethren of Anglo-Saxon or Celtic origin. It is not of these, however, that I desire to speak, excepting as an off-set to the unjust clamor against the so-called "Hessians", but of Germans, that were in the French auxiliary army, which came to America to aid this country in its struggle for independence.

A great deal of praise has been bestowed upon France, and deservedly, for the support it gave to the Colonies; and a warm affection has ever since been maintained by us toward that country. Yet France, it will be admitted, acted at the time simply on purely selfish motives. Thus says Carlo Botta, the celebrated Italian historian, who has written the best history of the American Revolutionary war, and who himself lived in, and was a citizen of France at the time of his writing: "Nor should we omit to say, that, though France would rather see America independent, than reconciled with England, she relished the prospect of a long war between them, still better than independence. Perhaps even, she would have best of all liked a conquest by dint of arms, and the consequent subjugation; for upon this hypothesis the English Colonies, ravaged and ruined, would have ceased to enrich the mother country in peace and in time of war; the English would no longer have found in their Colonists those powerful auxiliaries, who so often had succored them with so much efficacy. Should the Colonies, though vanquished, preserve their ancient prosperity, then England would be constrained to maintain in them a part of her force, in order to prevent the revolts she would have continually to dread on the part of a people impressed with recollection of so many outrages and cruelties.[5]" And the Abbé Raynal, a Frenchman, writes on the same subject: "France began the war under inappreciable advantages. The place, the time, the circumstances, all were carefully chosen. Only after it had deliberately made its preparations, and sent its troops as best suited, did it appear on the field of battle. It had to contend with an enemy, that was already humiliated, enfeebled, and discouraged by domestic dissensions. The favors of the other nations were on its side, when it contended with the haughty and imperious people commonly called the tyrants of the oceans. Yet I deemed it but just, when the people of the United States celebrated the great event, which terminated the war that made them a free and independent people, the surrender of Cornwallis at Yorktown, that they invited the representatives of France to come over and take part in and enjoy with them the festival, which they celebrated in commemoration of that happy day. But when the French representatives that came over, perceiving that the American people conferred alike and equally deserved honors upon the representatives of one of the most meritorious officers of the American Revolution, the Baron von Steuben, who even more disinterestedly than General Lafayette had lent his arm to the cause of this country at the most gloomy time of the war, and who continued after the war with the people of America, becoming one of them, which by way of parenthesis, none of the French officers did – when these representatives of Lafayette, Rochambeau and the French nation acted the silly part they did towards the relatives of the General von Steuben, then we may, with propriety, call it to public notice that even part of that glory, for which the French nation has received due honors and credit, was earned by people of that very nation which they attempted to sneer at, in the persons of the 'officiers Prussiens', the German nation.[6]"

For more than two centuries prior to the reconstruction of the German Empire, France had, owing to the disruption of

Germany into small principalities, always numerous German troops in its employ, and nearly in every instance, it was German warriors against the armies of Imperial Germany, that helped to gain the victories for the arms of France.[7] Were it not the soldiers of the "Rheinbund" and of Westphalia that aided the great Napoleon in his wars against Austria and Prussia?[8] And was not his fate doomed, when the "Rheinbund" and Westphalia turned against him? From the days of Richelieu the French armies were always speckled with troops, battalions and regiments of German soldiers, not only from Alsace and Lorraine, but from all the small principalities of southwestern Germany.[9] For this reason we should not be surprised, that among the French auxiliary troops of the American Revolution there were likewise large bodies of German soldiers, who aided in gaining the glories achieved by the French arms in that war. I will only incidentally mention here, that Lafayette, when he visited France in 1779, brought among the 300 men recruited in that country, more than one-half Germans from Strasbourg, resp. from the Alsace, the Palatinate and Baden, to America, as can readily be seen from a muster-roll now in the state Archives of Pennsylvania at Harrisburg, from which I took a copy a few years ago.

When France, under the treaty of Versailles with the American colonies (6th of Febr. 1778), began the war with England, it again sought and obtained soldiers in the neighboring principalities of Germany. So-called capitulations, or treaties for the furnishing of auxiliary troops, were entered into with the potentates of the upper Rhenish country, and as a large number of soldiers were at that time unemployed and at the disposal of their sovereigns, on account of the peace of Teschen (1779), France readily obtained bodies of men from southern Germany, as England had obtained them from the north. Thus we find many regiments and battalions from the principalities of the Palatinate, Bavaria, Württemberg, Ansbach, Trier, Anhalt, Switzerland and other states, in the French service, who were fighting in every direction of the compass under the white lily-banner of France. But though these were indirectly aiding American independence, by compelling England to divide its energies and to fritter away its power in many directions, nevertheless they cannot interest us in the same manner, as those troops, that came to America and took active part in the war on this continent. These alone I have in view, and among them we find not only individual soldiers interspersed in the ranks of the various organizations, but complete and compact German bodies of men. Although I intend to treat only of one regiment in particular in my essay, yet we may glance over a list of the various troops of Germans, that fought in Rochambeau's and d'Estaing's armies. These were:

1. The "Royal German Regiment Zweibrücken" or Deux-Ponts (Zweibrücken = French, "Deux-Ponts" - English, "Two Bridges"). This regiment was commanded by the following officers:

Colonel, Prince Christian von Zweibrücken

Lieutenant Colonel, Prince Wilhelm von Zweibrücken

Major, Baron Eberhardt von Esebach

Chief of Staff, Captain Haake

The two Princes von Zweibrücken were the sons of Duke Christian IV of Pfalz-Zweibrücken-Birkenfeld (a small principality in southwestern Germany) and Maria Anna Comtesse de Forbach. The princes were ineligible to the succession of the principality owing to the it seems morganatic marriage, which the Duke Christian IV had entered into with their mother who was a celebrated beauty at the court of Marie Antoinette, and who, if Samuel Abbot Green is correct, was formerly a ballet dancer. Upon her marriage to the duke she was raised to the rank of a Comtesse de Forbach. This, however, according to Ledebur's encyclopedia of the nobility of the Prussian monarchy, and the *Genealogisches Taschenbuch der freiherrlichen Familien Deutschlands*, for the year 1857 (p.904), is questionable.[10] That she was a lady of fine accomplished manners, great distinction and a marked influence at the French court, is known. She was intimately befriended with Benjamin Franklin, feeling a great deal of interest on behalf of the American cause; and it was upon her personal solicitation that the regiment in question was assigned by the Duke, her husband, for the expedition to America, with her two sons in command. Benjamin Franklin, in a codicil to his will, bequeathing a crab-apple walking stick to General Washington, says of this lady: "if it (the walking stick) were a scepter, he (Washington) would have merited it and would receive it. It was a present from that excellent woman, Madame de Forbach, the dowager Duchess of Deux-Ponts, connected with some verses, which should go with it."

The principality of Pfalz-Zweibrücken fell at the death of Christian IV to the electorate of Bavaria, and was inherited by the two cousins of our American officers, first the elector Charles Augustus of Bavaria and after his death by his brother Maximilian Joseph, (who in 1805 became first King of

Bavaria, under the name of Maximilian I); the small principality of Birkenfeld falling to the Grandduchy of Oldenburg.

Prince Christian, the Colonel of our regiment, was afterwards Field-Marshal General of the Bavarian army, and as such commanded the Bavarian troops with great distinction in the unfortunate battle of Hohenlinden (December 3, 1800). He was born in the city of Zweibrücken in the Palatinate in the year 1752, and died in the city of Munich about the year 1823. Prince Wilhelm, his brother the Lieutenant-Colonel, was born in Zweibrücken in the year 1754 and died in Munich, where he was the commander of the Royal Guards (Königl. Hartschiere) and Major-General in the Bavarian army, in the year 1841. Of the latter descendants in the male line are still living in Bavaria under the title of "Barons von Zweibrücken."

2. A battalion of Grenadiers from the electorate of Trier detached from the regiment "Saar." This body appears as "Detachement du regiment 'La Sarre'", and was incorporated into the regiment "Saintonge" commanded by the Count Adam Philip de Custine, the afterwards famous Marechal-de Camp (Field Marshal) of France, who during the French revolution commanded the victorious armies of that country

in Germany and later the "North-Army" in Flandres. Meeting the displeasure of Marat and Billand-Varenne, he was upon their accusation recalled, imprisoned, and three days thereafter executed on the guillotine (28 August 1793). Count Custine was born in the city of Metz, Febr. 4, 1740. His home was in the parish of Breisach in Alsace.

3. Two battalions of German Chasseurs (Jäger) from Alsace-Lorraine, of which one each was added to the regiments "Bourbonnais" and "Soisonnais."

4. Fully one-half of the legion of the Duke de Lanzun were Germans from Alsace, the Palatinate and Switzerland. I possess likewise a muster-roll of this legion copied from the original in the state Archives from Pennsylvania at Harrisburg, to prove my assertion.

5. It is doubtful, whether there were any bodies of German auxiliary troops in the army of the Count d'Estaing, but a regiment "Anhalt" of 600 strong is mentioned as taking part in the siege of Savannah. More definite facts are, however, not in my possession. The Count de Stedingk, born Oct. 26, 1746 in Castle Pinnow, near Greifswald in Pomerania, was in that unlucky affair the second in command of the French troops. It is possible that the regiment "Anhalt" belonged to this brigade. Count Stedingk was a bold warrior,

and his part taken in the storming of the Spring-hill redoubt was of the most daring and heroic nature. He planted the American flag on the most advanced position, however, being but very poorly supported by d'Estaing, was driven back with the loss of nearly one half of his command. As a recognition of his valor, he was decorated by Louis XVI with the order of the Knights of St. Louis, and was made a Field-Marshal of France. In 1787, however, he quit the French service and entered the army of the King of Sweden as a general. Since then he became a well-known diplomat of that power. He died at Stockholm in the year 1836.

6. Among the staff-officers of Rochambeau's army there were many German officers of distinction. The Count Axel von Fersen, a descendant of an old Pomeranian family of nobles, and the intimate friend of the Count Stedingk was Chief of Staff, and the Baron Ludwig von Closen-Haydenburg, born at Vlissingen in Holland, was one of the Adjutants-General to Rochambeau. The chief of Artillery was Captain Gau, formerly a Prussian officer and a German Professor. Lutz from Strasbourg accompanied the army as Rochambeau's interpreter. Two of the adjutants to the Baron de Viomesnil, the second in command, were the Barons Carl von Anselme, who fell as a Prussian officer in the battle of

Loan, March 10, 1814 and Paul Frederick Julius von Gambs, afterwards a prominent Judge of the Appellate Court in Bohemia, Austria. – All these officers were members of the American order of the Cincinnati, and received the badges from General Washington in person.

The effective strength of Rochambeau's army consisted of four regiments: "Bourbonnais", "Soisonnais", "Saintonge", and "Zweibrücken", each regiment about twelve hundred strong, or 800 men line and 400 men grenadiers and chasseurs; the Legion of the Duke de Lanzun was about 600 strong; and 200 men artillery, making a total of about 5600 men. According to nationality it may be divided as follows: One regiment, the "Zweibrücken", was entirely German, the three battalions of Grenadiers and Chasseurs were also Germans, one-half the Legion of the Duke de Lanzun, and all of the Artillery which, as we will further on see, was commanded in German, were likewise of that nationality. Thus we may safely assume that the rank and file of Rochambeau's army was about equally composed of French and Germans, if, indeed, the latter did not predominate. However, as I have already said before, I will only treat of the services of the purely German regiment, the "Zweibrücken", as far as that may be separated from the general actions of the entire French auxiliary army.

When the Franco-American alliance had been closed (1778), France, in the beginning, confined its making war upon England to the attacking of the British Colonies in the Mediterranean and West Indies, until in 1779 Lafayette came to Europe to sue at the Court of Versailles for the more direct and energetic participation. With reluctance only were the propositions of Lafayette listened to, and when a concession was made, there was an indecision as to the number of troops to be sent. The Marquis d'Estaing and Lafayette asked for 12,000 men, and the court agreed upon sending 8,000 but when the army arrived at Brest, it was found that means of transport were insufficient, and two regiments, one French, the regiment "Neustrie," and one German, the regiment "Anhalt" had to be left behind. As commander of the expedition the Marquis de Rochambeau was selected, not because he was a favorite at the court, but on account of his being well liked in the army.

On the 15th of April 1780 the fleet set sail for America. The original intentions were to sail to South Carolina, there to participate in the operations of General Lincoln, who was besieged by the British in Charleston; but on the arrival in the waters of that state, they learned from an English vessel captured by them, that Charleston had already fallen into the hands of the British by a capitulation of Gen. Lincoln and his forces. This caused the commander to change his course towards the north, and on the 11th of July the French fleet arrived in the harbor of Newport, R.I., where the troops were landed. The French were welcomed by the people of Newport with great joy, and at night the city was illuminated in honor of the arrival of the allies, though the Prince Wilhelm von Zweibrücken wrote in his journal that they were but coldly received: "We did not meet with that reception on landing," he says, "which we expected and which we ought to have had. A coldness and a reserve appear to me to be the characteristic of the American nation. They seem to have little of that enthusiasm which one supposes would belong to a people fighting for its liberties, and to be little suited to inspire it in others. But these considerations shall not at all change my resolution, and they occupy my thoughts less than my reflections upon our military and political position."

After landing the army, they entrenched themselves between Newport and Connecticut, against a threatened surprise from Lord Clinton, who occupied New York at the time. However beyond the mere threat, nothing serious was undertaken on the part of the British to disturb them, and in the latter part of October the army went into winter quarters in Newport and Providence, with the exception of Lanzun's legion, which took up quarters at Lebanon, Conn.

The winter passed away under festivities, arranged by the officers, to which the American officers and prominent citizens were invited, and which were often returned, and the performing of the regular duties on the part of the soldiers, in order to keep up the efficiency of the army. During this time the two Princes von Zweibrücken accompanied by the Count de Custine and the Marquis de Laval undertook a trip into the interior of the country, visiting Boston and other places, from which they returned on the 18th of January 1781. On March 6th Gen. Washington paid them a visit in Newport and was received with the honors of a Marshall of France, and upon his departure on the 13th of the same month the same honors were paid him. He held a grand review over the entire army and navy, and expressed his delight on account of the celerity and precision with which the maneuvers were performed.

A consultation as to the plans of the coming campaign with a view of a concerted action of the two armies was undoubtedly the principal object of Gen. Washington's visit. How these plans would develop, was at the time not yet clear.

As an immediate result we find that an expedition to Virginia by a detachment of the French fleet and army was undertaken, unquestionably with the intention to aid Gen. Lafayette in his enterprise of capturing Benedict Arnold, the traitor, who was then devastating the "Old Dominion" with fire and sword. For this purpose a part of the French fleet, with two companies of chasseurs from each of the four regiments, and about one-half of the Duke de Lanzun's legion on board, all under the command of Baron de Viomesnil, sailed from Newport on the 8th of March. The Marquis de Laval, the Vicomte de Noailles and the Barons von Anselme and von Gambs were the higher officers under him, the Chevalier Destouches commanding the fleet.

The British, however, had received information of the expedition, and so Admiral Arbuthnot, to counteract their intention, sailed about the same time from New York harbor. The two fleets met in the vicinity of Cape Henry, where a naval engagement took place, resulting in a drawn battle, which caused the Chevalier Destouches to return to Newport without having been able to disembark the land troops as projected. Thus Arnold escaped the greater danger of his life, for the fate that awaited him, had the Americans succeeded in his capture, would not have been uncertain. As Botta expresses it, "they would have buried the one of his legs, which had been wounded in the cause of the colonies while in their service with all the honors of war, and have hanged the rest of him."

The energies now developed in Virginia were of an extraordinary nature. Not only was Arnold's army, which originally had been opposed by the Baron von Steuben with an inferior force, strengthened by a division under General Philips, as an offset to Gen. Lafayette's command, which had marched from West Point early in February, but Lord Cornwallis, who in the previous year had disposed of the American army under Gen. Lincoln in South Carolina, marched his forces thither, thus concentrating one of the largest armies of the war in that state. The forces under Steuben and Lafayette were entirely inadequate, and Gen. Greene, who operated in North Carolina, was too far distant to be of any service. This enabled Cornwallis, who assumed the command when he entered Virginia, to press into the very heart of the state, placing the patriotic population of that commonwealth in the most critical position they had as yet experienced since the beginning of the war, so that Jefferson, then Governor, addressed himself in person to General Washington for relief.

On May 21, 1781 a conference was held between Generals Washington, Knox and du Portail on the part of the Americans, and Rochambeau and the Marquis de Chastellux on the part of the French, at Weathersfield, Conn., where the coming campaign was discussed. They united upon a combined siege of Lord Clinton in New York, and the French army at once broke camp, marching to Peekskill on the Hudson, where the Americans were encamped. For the purpose of making the siege effective, Gen. Washington called upon the Governors of the northern Colonies, asking them to speedily furnish their respective quotas assigned to them by Congress, in the whole 6,200 men. In the meantime another expedition of the French fleet should sail for Virginia, bringing succor to Gen. Lafayette, who was heavily pressed by Cornwallis in Yorktown.

The rest of May and the beginning of the month of June were consumed in the uniting of the two armies on the Hudson, and the preparation for the siege. Several reconnaissances were undertaken to the north of New York, and a camp was established on the Jersey Heights and well entrenched for the reception of the main army. Batteaux were built at Albany for the transport of 5,000 men down the Hudson, and on the 21st of July a reconnaissance in force was undertaken along the entire line of the British army. On the Jersey side of the North River reconnaissances were likewise made and opposite of Staten Island ovens were built for the intended use of the French army.

After this all had been successfully accomplished, the army again took up its encampment at White Plains, to await the arrival of the new levies. The colonies were however so derelict in the performance of their duties that General Washington, in a letter dated August 2, 1781 expressed himself on the situation as follows: "I am at this advanced time no stronger than I was when the army left winter quarters. Not a single man joined me, excepting 176 militia from Connecticut, who arrived at West Point yesterday, and 800 men of the New York levies, together with 200 men Connecticut State-troops; but these two divisions stood already on the line before the breaking up of winter quarters." This indeed melancholy, nay criminal negligence on the part of the Northern colonies, which might have brought them to the verge of ruin, was the unknown cause of the hastening of the final success of the war. General Clinton, convinced by the actions of the allied forces in his front, that their operations were intended for him, sent dispatch after dispatch to Lord Cornwallis, asking him for aid. Besides, on the 11th of August there appeared a fresh supply of German troops, in all 2,988 men, so that the garrison of New York had now a superior force to that of the allies. In addition to this, the news came in on the 14th of the same month, that the Count de Grasse had arrived in the American waters with a re-enforcement of the French fleet and army, the latter a brigade under the command of the Marquis de St. Simon; but that de Grasse had taken his course towards the Chesapeake Bay, declining to assist in a siege of New York, all very weighty reasons to compel Gen. Washington to a change of operations.

The new plan adopted was as follows: Instead of a siege of New York, the army should hasten in forced marches to Virginia, there to attack Cornwallis; but the appearance of a siege of Lord Clinton in New York should to the last moment be preserved, in order to prevent the pursuit and harassing of the army on its march as well as to detain Clinton from re-enforcing Cornwallis by way of the sea. Washington kept his plans so profoundly secret, that his own army, when he organized for a false demonstration on New York and a real movement of Yorktown, was unable to penetrate them. On the 19th of August they broke camp at White Plains. "We do not know the object of our march," writes the Prince Wilhelm von Zweibrücken, "and are in perfect ignorance, whether we are going against New York, or whether we are going to Virginia to attack Lord Cornwallis, who now occupies Portsmouth with a considerable force."

On the 22nd of August the army began the crossing of the Hudson River, which was completed on the 24th, the brigades of the Marquis de Rochambeau consolidating the rear. Demonstrative threats of an attack on New York were constantly made while the army marched to the South on the Jersey shore of the Hudson. Batteaux were carried on wagons to impress the enemy with the idea that Washington would attempt a crossing to Staten Island either from Elizabeth or Perth Amboy. However on the 26th the entire army was already on its march towards Philadelphia. In vain did the Hessian Colonel von Wurmb, who commanded at Kingsbridge, report to Clinton again and again, that the allied army made preparations for a march against Cornwallis; Clinton was deaf to all arguments and would not be diverted from his opinion, that the movements of the allies were but strategems to draw his army out of New York. Alas! On the 2nd of September it began to dawn upon the British commander, that Washington might have wended his way to the south. It was then too late to remedy the error.

Washington, indeed, had skillfully deceived even his own men. As late as August 26th, Prince Wilhelm von Zweibrücken writes in his journal: "Today we marched to Pompton. The army of Gen. Washington is separated from us, and had the appearance of going to Paulus Hook or towards Staten Island. I cannot make up my mind as to the object of our march. I am inclined to believe that the Americans will attack one of the two points which they are threatening, and I am quite certain, they will not act without us." [11] But already on the next day the question was solved for the prince, when he learned from one of his friends, however in the strictest secrecy, that all the maneuvers by which they threatened New York, were only feints, and that Lord Cornwallis was the real object of their arms.

While the allies were marching, the royalists in New York were amusing themselves over the following news, unquestionably prepared to lull Lord Clinton in careless indolence: "A gentleman," writes *Rivington's Royal Gazette* of August 25th, "just arrived from Jersey informs us, that young Laurens lately passed through that province on his return from Paris and has brought the following very interesting intelligence, that the Emperor of Germany had declared himself the ally of Great Britain (all in large capitals), which threw the Court of Versailles into much confusion, as a consequence of this great event, the French nation must withdraw all support from their new allies, the rebels of this continent; and we are informed it has, with another concurring circumstance, occasioned Mr. Washington and the Count Rochambeau to quit their menacing position at White Plains. We are also told that the French Admiral is embarking all the sick troops on board of his squadron, from which it is suggested that their fleet and army are to be withdrawn from Rhode Island, to strengthen themselves in the West Indies. It is said that the French and rebels left their ground the day after Mr. Washington received the mortifying account of the Emperor's alliance with his old friend, the Court of Great Britain." It is plain, that this information was only a well prepared ruse to deceive Clinton, and it was really surprising how easily he allowed himself to be duped by such shallow news.

The march of the allies was hastened as fast as possible. On the 1st of September they passed through Trenton, on the 3rd they arrived at Philadelphia where the army rested one day, on which occasion they paraded before Congress. On the 5th while they camped at Chester, they learned the authentic news of the arrival of Admiral de Grasse with 28 sails of the line in the Chesapeake Bay and that an auxiliary army under St. Simon had safely landed on the 28th of August with orders to unite with the corps of Gen. Lafayette, "the joy which this welcome news produces among all the troops," writes Prince Wilhelm, "which penetrates Gen. Washington and the Count de Rochambeau, is more easy to feel than to express. The moment which is to be the recompense of our hardships, of our fatigues, and of our absence draws near, and I hope, that we shall enjoy it." A note which the prince adds to his journal on this occasion, characteristic of Gen. Washington, is very interesting: "I am equally surprised and touched," writes he, "at the true and pure joy of General Washington. Of a natural coldness and of a serious and noble approach, which in him is only true dignity, and which adorns so well the chief of a whole nation, his features, his physiognomy, his deportment – all were changed in an instant. He put aside his character as arbiter of North America and contented himself for the moment with that of a citizen, happy at the good fortune of his country. A child, whose every wish had been gratified, would not have experienced a sensation more lively, and I believe that I am doing honor to the feelings of this rare man, in endeavoring to express all their ardor."

Let me here skip the uninteresting details of the march of the allied army, and resume again by narrating the interesting acts connected with the siege of Yorktown.

On September 26th they arrived at Williamsburg, where the entire army, including the corps of Lafayette, von Steuben and St. Simon, were united. Two days later the march was again resumed, and in the afternoon the troops arrived before Yorktown, where Lord Cornwallis was strongly entrenched and fortified. A mile from the town the army separated into brigades, and the siege of the place began at once; the American forming the right wing, leaning on Wormleys Creek and York River below the town, whilst the French took position on the left, with the Marquis de St. Simon leaning on York River above. Gloucester Point, on the opposite shore of the river, was besieged by the American General Wieden, who commanded 1,200 men (according to others 2,000) Virginia militia, and the Duke de Lanzun's corps, supported by the legion of Colonel Armand, total about 3,000 or 4,000 men.[12]

Where, as we have seen, the joys over the safe arrival of the Count de Grasse in the waters of Virginia were great, the rejoicings over the happy junction of the several parts of the army and the navy, now firmly besieging one of the grand bodies of the English army, were truly exuberant. Washington, Rochambeau and some of the superior officers, hastening ahead of the army, were formally received by the Count de Grasse on board of the French flag-ship "Ville de Paris" on the 17th of September. After that time, festivals were arranged by the light-minded and frolicsome French officers almost daily, to which the American officers were, of course, invited.

The French were able thus to relieve the monotony of the camp life by the arrangements of jollifications, for they had received with the fleet of de Grasse a full year's pay and other funds, over 1,800,000 francs but the American officers, poor and destitute even of almost immediate necessities, were unable to return the compliments, which caused Gen. Lafayette to arrange so-called American dinners in order that he might shine as the patron of the American corps of officers, for which, it is true, he was well fitted, having been supplied by the fleet with abundant means from France. Vexed at the idea, that Lafayette should have the monopoly of this, the Baron von Steuben arranged likewise a grand dinner, and it is said, that he sold his service plate and his horse and even pawned away his orders, to obtain the necessary funds for that purpose.

Amid these festivities, however, the siege was not neglected. On the 29th of September the American army advanced its lines across Wormleys creek, to tighten the siege. During the night following, the English abandoned two of their outer redoubts, which were in front of the right wing of the French army. The Marquis de Rochambeau, accompanied by the Prince Wilhelm von Zweibrücken and the Baron von Steuben whose command, consisting of the Pennsylvania, Virginia and Maryland line, adjoined the French brigade "Bourbonnais", composed of the regiments "Bourbonnais" and "Zweibrücken", forming together the center of the siege-army, made an inspection of the abandoned works. The Prince expressed his surprise that the British should have abandoned these redoubts, by the holding of which, although the works were not strong in themselves, they might have harassed their adversaries for many days, compelling them to their capture by tedious approaches, thus prolonging the siege for some time.

On the 6th of October, when all the necessary preparations were completed the fascines, gabions, hurdles and soucissons being ready, almost all the siege guns having arrived and the plans for the trenches were settled upon - General Washington gave the order to open the first parallel, which was begun that very night. This parallel was placed within 600 paces from the works of the enemy. The Americans began the trenches on the right and the French on the left, and in three days they were completed and provided with the necessary batteries, all manned with mortars and heavy siege-guns. The French and the Americans vied with each other in their work, and so well was this done, that General Washington acknowledged his gratification in a general order. Already on the 9th of October the mortars and siege-guns could begin the destruction of the enemy's works. In the night of the 10th, the British man of war "Charon" with 44 guns was set on fire with hot shot from a star-work erected in the meantime by the regiment "Touraine" on the left wing of the French army.

On the 11th of October the second parallel was begun by the allied forces. It was advanced to within 300 yards of the enemy's works. On the part of the French the regiments "Zweibrücken" and "Gatenois" - the latter being one of the regiments of the brigade under the Marquis de St. Simon - were detailed on this occasion to the perilous duty in the trenches. The British, however, had no idea of the work which threatened their ruin, and only on the next morrow, when the labors were so far advanced, that the men were sufficiently protected in the ditches did the outpost of the English army discover the work that had been done during the night. They at once began to pour in a torrent of bombs and shot but of no avail, for the guns of the first parallel soon opened such heavy and well directed fire, that instead of preventing the progress of the new trenches, the English soon found their own batteries on their left completely demolished and silenced.

The second parallel now advanced rapidly towards completion. Only two redoubts on the left wing of the enemy interrupted their progress, for to be of effective service, the trenches necessarily had to be extended to York River. "As long as these two works belong to the enemy," writes the Prince von Zweibrücken, "our parallel will be imperfect; and we hope that they will be attacked at once."

On the 14th of October the regiments "Gatenois" and "Zweibrücken" were ordered into the trenches. When the latter assembled for duty, the Baron de Viomesnil, who on the part of the French was commander of the day, ordered the Prince Wilhelm von Zweibrücken to come to him on their arrival at the entrances of the trenches. Viomesnil then gave the order, that the Grenadiers and Chasseurs of the two regiments would be separated and formed into a battalion, to the command of which he assigned the Prince Wilhelm von Zweibrücken, telling him, that he thought he gave him thereby a proof of his esteem and confidence. "His words were not enigmatical to me," writes the Prince, "I was not mistaken as to the object for which he intended me. A moment afterwards he confirmed my opinion, telling me, that I should make the attack on one of the redoubts, which obstructed the continuation of our second parallel. He gave me orders to place my battalion under cover, and to wait until he should send for me to make with him a reconnaissance of the redoubt. In the course of the afternoon, he took me with the Baron de l'Estrade, lieutenant-colonel of the regiment "Gatenois", whom he had given me as second in command, and two sergeants from the grenadiers and chasseurs of my battalion, men as brave as they were intelligent, and who were charged particularly to reconnoiter with the strictest exactitude the road which we would have to follow during the night. We examined with the greatest care the object of the attack, and all the details.

The general explained very clearly to us his plans. --- He then ordered me at once to form my battalion, and to lead it to that part of the trenches nearest to which we ought to come out. I called together the captains of my battalion, and told them the duty with which we were honored. I had no occasion to excite their courage, nor that of the troops whom I commanded; but it was my duty to let them know the wishes of the General, and the exact order in which we were to attack the enemy."

The evening came. As the two redoubts were to be taken simultaneously, the one to the right by the Americans under Lafayette, and the one to the left by the command of the Prince von Zweibrücken, it was arranged that the firing of six shells should serve as the signal for the attack. I will now narrate this attack with the words of the Prince von Zweibrücken:

"The six shells were fired at last; and I advanced in the greatest silence. At a hundred and twenty or thirty paces, we were discovered, and the Hessian soldier who was stationed as a sentinel on the parapet, cried out "Wer da?" to which we did not reply, but hastened our steps. The enemy opened fire the instant after the "Wer da." We lost not a moment in reaching the Abatis, which being strong and well preserved, at about twenty-five paces from the redoubt, cost us many men, and stopped us for some minutes, but it was cleared away with brave determination. We threw ourselves into the ditch at once, and each one sought to break through the fraises and to mount the parapet. We got there at first in small numbers, and I gave the order to fire. The enemy kept us a sharp fire and charged us at bayonet-point, but no one was driven back. The carpenters, who had worked hard on their part, had made some breaches in the palisades, which helped the main body of troops in mounting. The parapet was becoming manned visibly. Our fire was increasing and making terrible havoc among the enemy, who had placed themselves behind a kind of barricade of barrels, where they were well massed, and where all our shots told. We succeeded at the moment, when I wished to give the order to leap into the redoubt and charge upon the enemy with the bayonet, then they laid down their arms, and we leaped in with more tranquility and less risk. I shouted immediately to cry "Vive le Roi," which was repeated by all the grenadiers and chasseurs, who were in good condition and by all the troops in the trenches; to which the enemy replied by a general discharge of artillery and musketry. I never saw a sight more beautiful or more majestic."

The redoubt which was stormed by the Prince von Zweibrücken was manned by about a hundred men Hessian troops and thirty men English grenadiers. The commander, McPherson, and the British soldiers, say the Prince, "saved themselves ignominiously" - the moment they discovered the attack, leaving the field to their German comrades to defend, who continued the fight with much bravery and inflicted upon the command of the Prince very severe losses.

Ninety-two men of the attacking party, among them five officers, were either killed or wounded, the Prince von Zweibrücken himself being among latter, having received a slight contusion on the head by a fragment of an exploded shell. The redoubt stormed by Lafayette offered no marked resistance and was surrendered by the British garrison immediately after the first attack.

It is remarkable, that in this important fight - the only fight of any note in which the army of Rochambeau took part in the entire war, and the only serious affair outside of the regular siege during the investment of Yorktown - it was Germans against Germans that stood opposed to each other; it is highly probable, that the grenadiers and chasseurs of the regiments "Gatenois" and "Agenois" were like those of the other regiments, also Germans, for the orders were given in the German language. Thus writes Eelking, copying from the journal of Johann Conrad Döhla, a Hessian subaltern officer, who was a participant in the affair on the British side: "During the attack the French and Americans used the following strategem: In the line of the attacking column as well as the centre we heard the commands given in German and loud: Die ganze Kolonne oder Brigade, vorwärts, Marsch! - Halt! - Kanonen vor! &c." (In column or brigade, forward march! - Halt! Cannons or artillery to the front! &c.) - Is it not plain that Döhla here mistook the fact for a strategem? When we know, that the centre was composed mainly of Germans - the regiment "Zweibrücken"; and adjoining brigades of Steuben, largely Pennsylvania, Maryland and Virginia Germans were forming the centre - and when we furthermore know, that the attacking column was at least one-half, if not entirely a German body, we may safely accept it as a fact, that it was German soldiers on both sides, that fought this sharply contested affair. But there are other witnesses. The Baron de Viomesnil, as commander of the whole, in his report to the Marquis de Rochambeau, speaks of the Prince von Zweibrücken, who commanded four hundred grenadiers or "chasseurs", "whom I intended for the attack on the grand redoubt, as well as M. de l'Estrade, lieutenant-colonel of the "Gatenois", whom I had placed under his orders, and in his advance guard, marched there with so much order and firmness, that they were not of six minutes in making themselves masters of the redoubt, and in manning it. This decisive attack has cost in all nearly one hundred men; but it will reflect the greatest honor on the Count Wilhelm von Zweibrücken, M. de l'Estrade, the Count of Rostaing and the officers and troops who have been engaged in it. There were joy and confidence before sallying out, silence, energy and difficulties overcome during the attack, much order and humanity after the success. General, this is what I have seen of the nation and Grenadiers von Zweibrücken, after twenty years of peace; and this is what I am happy to announce to you ... the Count Wilhelm has been wounded in the face, though slightly; his conduct has been so brilliant and his bravery so distinguished, and so decisive, that I pray you, General, to obtain for him from the favor of the King the rank of brigadier."

Was not the word nation, as applied to the Zweibrückers, there used in the sense of nationality? If so, then there can be no doubt, that Viomesnil in using the term 'Zweibrücken' meant German. The aged veteran journalist, Mr. L. A. Wollenweber, who now resides at Reading, Penn., himself a born Zweibrücker, writes me, that in his youth he was well acquainted with many of the officers and men, that had been in Rochambeau's army naming several, among them his own grand uncle on his mother's side, Louis Ambos, who died in

1824; that he was present at the funeral of the Baron von Esebeck, the Major of the regiment, who afterwards commanded the regiment, and who was a General under the first Napoleon, when the Palatinate, like the German provinces of Alsace and Lorraine, was incorporated in Imperial France; that he often, when a boy had heard the old veterans speak of their campaigns in America, and of their marches, and that he remembered distinctly, that they frequently remarked, that the large majority army, (meaning Rochambeau's) were Germans from the Palatinate and the neighboring country.[13] And finally, Bancroft, in his history of the American Revolution, states, that the German regiments in the British service- especially naming the "Ansbach" regiments - after they had laid down their arms, when they were passing in front of their regiment "Zweibrücken" going back to their quarters, forgot, that they stood in arms arrayed against each others, and that they embraced their countrymen with tears in their eyes, much to the chagrin of the British soldiers.[14] May we not assume that Bancroft commits an error here, by naming the regiment "Zweibrücken" when we know that this regiment was not then at all in line, but that it was still on duty in the trenches until the entire ceremony of capitulation was over, as we will presently see? And if so, is it not clear that there must have been other German troops in the French army, that were thus embraced by their countrymen? We know that at the time there were "Ansbach" troops in the French service, would it therefore not seem probable, that these were in the same manner incorporated into the regiments "Gatenois", "Agenois" and "Touraine" of St. Simon's army as the light infantry, grenadiers and chasseurs of those bodies as the Trierer and Alsacians were incorporated into the four regiments of Rochambeaus first army? Then the embracing of countrymen becomes more clear for it might have been neighbors and even relatives, that found themselves under such remarkable circumstances on the last of the American battlefields of the Revolutionary war. But to return to the narrative of our regiment: The Marquis de Rochambeau in his report likewise bestows the highest encomiums of praise upon the Prince von Zweibrücken and the soldiers under him, and orders, that two days extra pay and rations be distributed among the four companies of grenadiers and chasseurs of the regiments "Zweibrücken" and "Gatenois" besides the special allowances given to the sappers and carpenters, who ax in hand had cut the breaches in the palisades. Gen. Washington also recognizes in a general order the bravery of the four hundred heroes, who under the Prince Wilhelm had stormed the strong redoubt; and he presents the regiments "Zweibrücken" and "Gatenois" each with one of the two brass pieces of ordnance captured by them, "as a remembrance of the valour, with which they stormed the redoubt of the enemy in the night of the 15th inst.," which present was afterwards confirmed by Congress.

The importance of the capturing of these redoubts was felt at once. During the same night they were included into the second parallel, and from this moment the fate of the besieged garrison was doomed. True, the British made the faint attempt of a sally early in the morning of the 16th of October, but their efforts were in vain. On the morning of the 17th the regiments "Zweibrücken" and "Bourbonnais" went into the trenches on the part of the French and the division of the Baron von Steuben on the part of the Americans. The fire upon the enemy's works was now opened with such a vigor, that the British fortifications were presently, so to speak, entirely destroyed. "It was impossible to fire a gun from them," writes Stedman, "the palisades were demolished and in many places breeches were begun." All resistance now became hopeless, and as an attempt on the part of Lord Cornwallis to escape during the night across the York River having likewise failed, he offered a capitulation. "At ten o'clock in the morning," writes the Prince von Zweibrücken, "Lord Cornwallis sent a flag of truce to Gen. Washington, to decide the fate of the Garrisons of Yorktown and Gloucester, and to request a suspension of hostilities. From that moment they began to make arrangements for capitulation but they continued to fire until four o'clock, when by means of a new flag of truce, the firing stopped on both sides."

The negotiations lasted until the 19th of October, when the capitulation of the British forces of Yorktown and Gloucester was definitely agreed upon. The regiments "Bourbonnais" and "Royal Zweibrücken", writes Prince Wilhelm, "which were in the trenches when the negotiations began, were not relieved until after the ceremony of laying down their arms on the part of the enemy was over." On the part of the Americans the brigade of Pennsylvania (Wayne's), Virginia (Muehlenberg's) and Maryland (Gist's) which composed the division of the Gen. Steuben were likewise in the trenches, and refused to be relieved, which led to the well-known scene between Steuben and Lafayette, when the latter attempted with his division to enter the trenches on the 18th, which was refused on the part of the Baron, who contended that it was one of the rules of war that the troops on service, when the preliminaries of a surrender on the part of the enemy is offered, have the honor to remain in service until the surrender is completed.

At _____ on the morning of the 19th of October the articles for the surrender of York and Gloucester were signed. At 12 o'clock the British redoubts No. 7 and 8 on the left of their works were delivered, the one to the Americans, the others to the French, and occupied by the troops under the command of the Baron von Steuben and the Baron de Viomésnil, respectively, the Prince Wilhelm von Zweibrücken and General Anthony Wayne. The British banner with the cross of St. George sank and in its place appeared the American stars and stripes to float henceforth undisturbed over the land of the free. With the capitulation of Lord Cornwallis the war was virtually ended. The regiment "Zweibrücken" which had taken such prominent part in the last act of that war, had the honor (a German regiment) to plant the French flag upon the walls of Yorktown.[15]

1. The term "Hessian" was used with reference to the German troops allied with the British, although they were not all from Hessia. Also the term had negative connotations, and implied that the soldiers were inhumane "Huns" sent over to assist the British in the suppression of the Revolution. For general coverage of the period see the titles listed in endnote 2, as well as the following works: Rodney Atwood, *The Hessians: Mercenaries from Hessen-Kassel in the American Revolution.* (Cambridge: Cambridge University Press, 1980), and Joseph P. Tustin, ed., *Diary of the American War: A Hessian Journal.* (New Haven: Yale University Press, 1979). For reference to other works on the topic, see Margrit B. Krewson, *Von Steuben and the German Contribution to the American Revolution: A Selective Bibliography.* (Washington, D.C.: Library of Congress, 1987).

2. The works listed here are some of the basic sources on the topic: Friedrich Kapp, *Der Soldatenhandel deutscher Fürsten nach Amerika. Ein Beitrag zur Kulturgeschichte des achtzehnten Jahrhunderts* . 2. verm und umgearb. Aufl. (Berlin: J. Springer, 1874); George Bancroft, *History of the United States of America: From the Discovery of the Continent to 1789.* (New York: Appleton, 1882-84), 6 vols.; George Washington Greene, *The German Element in the War of American Independence.* (New York: Hurd & Houghton, 1876); and Edward Jackson Lowell, *The Hessians and Other German Auxiliaries of Great Britain in the Revolutionary War.* (Port Washington, NY: Kennikat Press, 1965), and Don Heinrich Tolzmann, ed., *The German-American Soldier in the Wars of the U.S.: J. A. Rosengarten's History.* (Bowie, MD: Heritage Books, Inc., 1996).

3. See Max von Eelking, *The German Allied Troops in the North American War of Independence, 1776-1783.* (1893,

Reprint: Bowie: Heritage Books, Inc., 1987).

4. Regarding the German role in the Revolution, see Tolzmann, *The German-American Soldier,* pp.54ff. Regarding Zweibruecken, see pp.83, 115, 176.

5. See Carlo Botta, *History of the War of the Independence of the United States of America.* (New Haven: W. Whiting, 1837).

6. See Abbé Raynal, *The Revolution of America*, 2nd Edinburgh ed., with a New Introduction and Preface by George Athan Billias. (Boston: Gregg Press, 1972).

7. Regarding the history of Germany in this time period, see Geoffrey Barraclough, *The Origins of Modern Germany.* (Oxford: F. Blackwell, 1947).

8. Regarding the Rheinbund, or the Confederation of the Rhine, see Hajo Holborn, *The History of Modern Germany.* (Princeton: Princeton University Press, 1982), especially vol. 2.

9. Regarding the role of Germans in the French army, see Steven T. Ross, *French Military History, 1661-1799: A Guide to the Literature.* (New York: Garland, 1984). German soldiers were serving in the French military due to the fact that after the Thirty Years War, France took possession of the German provinces of Alsace and Lorraine. Also, see Don Heinrich Tolzmann, ed., *German Allied Troops in the American Revolution: J. A. Rosengarten's History* (Bowie, MD: Heritage Books, Inc., 1993), especially pp.32-36, which deals with German troops in the French military during the American Revolution.

10. See Leopold Karl Wilhelm August Freiherr von Ledebur, *Adelslexikon der preussischen Monarchie*. (Berlin: Rauh, 1854-56) and *Gothaisches genealogisches Taschenbuch* . . . (Gotha: Julius Perthes, 1857).

11. For further information on Zweibrücken and its role in the American Revolution, see Karl Theodor von Heigel, *Die Beteiligung des Hauses Zweibrücken am nordamerikanischen Befreiungskrieg*. (München: Verlag der Königlich Bayerischen Akademie der Wissenschaften, 1912). For a general history of Zweibrücken, see Johann Georg Lehmann, *Vollständige Geschichte des Herzogtums Zweibrücken und seiner Fürsten*. (München: C. Kaiser, 1867).

12. Regarding Gerhard von der Wieden and Armand's Legion, see Tolzmann, *German-Americans in the American Revolution,* pp.515, 536.

13. L.A. Wollenweber was a well-known 19th century German-American author. See his *Gemälde aus dem pennsylvanischen Volksleben: Schilderungen und Aufsätze in poetischer und prosaischer Form, in Mundart und Ausdrucksweise der Deutsch-Pennsylvanier.* (Philadelphia: Schaefer & Koradi, 1869).

14. See Bancroft, History of the United States of America.

15. With regard to the Battle of Yorktown, see Albert B. Faust, *The German Element in the U.S.* (New York: Steuben Society of America, 1927), vol. I, pp.246-47.

Part Three - Editor's Conclusion

Editor's Conclusion

According to Rattermann, there was an "even greater number of Germans who fought and shed their life blood upon the battlefields of American Independence, and for the liberties of the country, than the number of unfortunate Germans, that were forced to fight in the British ranks." In short, the number of German-Americans and Germans who fought for Independence may have been greater than the number of the Germans who fought with the British. We know that the number of the latter was ca. 30,000, or one-third of the British forces.[1]

The German-American involvement has already been known to have been crucial in a statistical sense, as it is commonly estimated that one-third of the colonists were for the Revolution, one-third were Tory, and one-third neutral, whereas German-Americans were considered to have been up to 90% in support of the Revolution, as England was not their mother country, and they felt absolutely no sense of loyalty to Britain. An example of their statistical importance can readily been seen by examining the colonies where Germans were concentrated.

For example, in Pennsylvania where one-third of the colony was English and one-third German, and the remainder a mixture of various other groups, it can readily be seen that if roughly one-third of the English, who were one-third of the population, supported the Revolution, then having up to 90% of the one-third that was German, would be of great importance in terms of Pennsylvania's support of the struggle.

One item illuminating the support of German-Americans in Pennsylvania was that on 4 July 1776, when the delegates of 53 battalions met in Lancaster to choose a Brigadier-General, a full one-third were German-American.[2]

These kinds of considerations lend merit to the assertion of Rattermann that the American forces may have had a larger German contingent than the British forces. Does this possibly mean that the American Army may have been roughly one-third German-American/German? This factor has previously never been considered in works dealing with the American Revolution, as the German contingent did not include the German troops serving with the French. It is a question in need of further exploration and examination.

Elsewhere, I have discussed the importance of the German-American involvement in the American Revolution, and made reference to the fact that three of the most important positions in the American Continental Army were held by German-Americans: Inspector-General (Baron von Steuben), Quartermaster-General (Heinrich Lutterloh), and Superintendent of Baking (Christopher Ludwig). Also, other prominent military leaders have been discussed, such as Baron DeKalb, Peter Muhlenberg, Nicholas Herkimer, etc., as examples of the leadership roles played by German-Americans.[3] Reference has also been made to the German-American regiments and units, which were formed.

However, the role played by German-Americans has never been placed together with that of the Germans who fought with them in the service of the French. Together, they formed a major segment of the Continental Army.

This sheds a completely new light on the role played by the German contingent in the American Revolution. On the basis of these considerations, it becomes clear that the German-American/German role in the American Revolution was on a statistical basis alone an essential element in the struggle for American Independence.

This work, therefore, is of great importance in further illuminating our understanding of the American Revolution, and in demonstrating the important role played by German-Americans in the War of Independence. It is hoped that this work will contribute to a greater appreciation of this role, and that this will in the future be reflected in works dealing with the American Revolution.

1. See Don Heinrich Tolzmann, ed., *German Allied Troops in the American Revolution: J. G. Rosengarten's Survey of German Archives and Sources* (Bowie, MD: Heritage Books, Inc., 1993)

2. See Don Heinrich Tolzmann, *America's German Heritage*. (Cleveland: German-American National Congress, 1976).

3. Ibid. Also, see Don Heinrich Tolzmann, ed., *German-Americans in the American Revolution: Henry Melchior Richards' History*. (Bowie, MD: Heritage Books, Inc., 1993).

Index

Anselme, Carl von, 16, 21
Antoinette, Marie, 12
Arbuthnot, Admiral, 21
Armand, Colonel, 29
Arnold, Benedict, 19, 20
Atwood, Rodney, 48
Bancroft, George, 4, 42, 48
Barraclough, Geoffrey, 49
Billand-Varenne, 14
Botta, Carlo, 6, 49
Bull, John, 3
Chastellux, Marquis de, 23
Christian IV, Duke, 12, 13
Clinton, Lord, 23, 24, 27-29
Closen-Haydenburg, Baron Ludwig von, 16
Cornwallis, Lord, 8, 22, 23, 25-27, 30, 46
Custine, Adam Philip de, 14
DeKalb, General, 5, 55
Destouches, Chevalier, 21
Döhla, Johann Conrad 39, 40
d'Estaing, Count, 15, Marquis, 18
Eelking, Capt. Max von, 4, 39, 49
Esebach, Baron Eberhardt von, 11
Faust, Albert B., 50
Fersen, Count Axel von, 16
Forbach, Maria Anna Comtesse de, 12, 13
Franklin, Benjamin, 12

Gambs, Paul Frederick Julius von, 16, 21
Gau, Captain, 16
Gist, 45
Grasse, de, 25, 29, 31
Green, Samuel Abbot, 12
Greene, George W., 4, 22
Haake, Capt., 11
Heigel, Karl Theodor von, 50
Herkimer, Nicholas, 55
Hoffmann, John, xii
Holborn, Hajo, 49
Jefferson, 22
Joseph, Maximilian, 13
Kapp, Frederick, 4, 48
Knox, 23
Krewson, Margrit B., 48
Lafayette, 8, 10, 18, 21-23, 29, 32, 37, 39, 46
Lanzun, Duke de, 15, 17, 20, 21, 31
Laurens, 27
Laval, Marquis de, 21
Ledebur, 12
Lehmann, Johann Georg, 50
Lincoln, Gen., 18
Louis XVI, 15
Lowell, Edward Jackson, 4
Ludwig, Christopher, 55
Lutterloh, Heinrich, 55
Lutz, 16
l'Estrade, Baron de, 36, 40, 41
Marat, 14

McPherson, 38
Muehlenberg, 5, 45
Muhlenberg, Peter, 55
Napoleon, 9, 42
Noailles, Vicomte de, 21
Pfalz-Zweibrücken, 13
Philips, Gen., 22
Portail, Gen. du, 23
Richelieu, 9
Rattermann, H. A., vii, xi, 53
Raynal, Abbé, 7, 49
Richards, Henry Melchior Muhlenberg, xi
Rochambeau, 8, 16-18, 23, 26, 28, 29, 31, 32, 39, 41, 42
Rosengarten, J. A., 48, 49
   J. G., xi, 3, 10
Ross, Steven T., xii, 49
Rostaing, 41
St. Simon, Marquis de 30, 31
Sell, Donna-Christine, xi
Stedingk, Count de, 15, 16
Stedman, 45
Steuben, Baron, von, 5, 8, 22, 30, 32, 40, 45, 46, 48, 55
Tolzmann, Don Heinrich, xi, 6, 9, 31, 48, 49, 57
Tustin, Joseph P., 48
Viomesnil, Baron de, 21, 35, 40
Walle, Dennis Francis, xi
Washington, General, 13, 16, 20, 23-31, 33, 44, 45

Wayne, Anthony, 45, 46
Wieden, General, 31
Wollenweber, L. A., 41, 50
Wurmb, Colonel von, 26
Young, Dorothy, x
Zweibrücken, 13
   Christian von, x, 11, 12, 20
   Wilhelm von, 11-13 19, 20, 26, 27, 29, 32, 35, 37, 38, 39, 40, 41, 45, 46

www.ingramcontent.com/pod-product-compliance
Lightning Source LLC
Chambersburg PA
CBHW071230160426
43196CB00012B/2470